THE POWER OF THE TONGUE

Pernell Stoney

Copyright © 2014 by Pernell Stoney

The Power of The Tongue
by Pernell Stoney

Printed in the United States of America

ISBN 9781628718751

All rights reserved solely by the author. The author guarantees all contents are original and do not infringe upon the legal rights of any other person or work. No part of this book may be reproduced in any form without the permission of the author. The views expressed in this book are not necessarily those of the publisher.

Unless otherwise indicated, Scriptures are taken from the King James Version of the Bible.

Scripture quotations marked TLB are taken from The Living Bible. Copyright © 1971. Used by permission of Tyndale House Publishers, Inc., Carol Stream, Illinois 60188. All rights reserved.

Scripture quotations marked RSV are from the Revised Standard Version of the Bible. Copyright © 1946, 1952, and 1971 by the Division of Christian Education of the National Council of the Churches of Christ in the United States of America. Used by permission. All rights reserved.

Scripture quotations marked NKJV are taken from the New King James Version®. Copyright © 1982 by Thomas Nelson, Inc. Used by permission. All rights reserved.

www.xulonpress.com

CONTENTS

Introduction vii
Acknowledgments ix
Dedication xi

Chapter 1: The Power of the Tongue 13
Chapter 2: Life and Death 20
Chapter 3: The Things We Say 28
Chapter 4: The Things People Say to Us 41
Chapter 5: The Forces of Good vs. the Forces
    of Evil 54
Chapter 6: Life and Death 63
Chapter 7: A Perfect Creation 70
Chapter 8: Why Did You Say That? 80
Chapter 9: Upgrades for Download 86
Chapter 10: Praying God's Way 95

Closing Thoughts and Prayer 99

INTRODUCTION

Men and women of the world—believers and unbelievers alike—lack the knowledge of what they are saying and the effect it has on their lives and on the lives of others. Tragically, this lack of knowledge is taught daily on television shows, at the movies, on the streets, at home, and, yes, even in the church. Men are teaching their sons and daughters negative language, something for them to aspire to when they grow up. These words come from a lack of understanding that what is said can really affect them. The bottom line: Satan has deafened their ears to the power of words. If God's people would study His Word (we are all God's people; we just have to accept Him), they would come to know that the things we say determine how we get there and what we become. Our present actions are far from honoring God with our lifestyle. As men and women of God, we need to renew our thought patterns through the Word of God. His Word will teach us the ingredients we need to honor Him and be positive when we speak.

Our children are lost because they don't see the Spirit of God in their parents or their friends. Though all of us are here in the flesh, we need to get filled with the Spirit of God. In this book, you will be presented with Scriptures from the Old and New Testaments that will prove to you that God wants you to be positive in your speaking, developing a relationship with Him and loving one another. As you read about part of my eye-opening, life-changing experience, I hope it will change you the way it has changed me. I pray to God that you will hear what He is saying to you and be able to experience the great joy of being open and obedient to our Lord and Savior.

ACKNOWLEDGMENTS

First, I give thanks and honor to my Lord and Savior, Jesus Christ. It is through His blood that I am saved. Thanks go to my wife, Hwason, for still loving me after thirty-four years of bad and good times. She is a true friend and a woman of God. My gratitude also goes to my daughter, Cherry, one of the sweetest people you could ever meet, who is always thinking of others first, and to my son, Steven, a man with strong family values, who is always in my heart with a love that is unmatched.

Thanks go to my spiritual families, Pastor James, GiGi, and DD Williams, and Minister Johnny, Robin, and Moses Williams. We love you with the love of God. God has given all of you a heart of love and caring. Thanks for being there for us. Thanks go to Dr. Michael and Brineta Mitchell, my pastors, mentors, and longtime friends of Restoration Ministries International (RMI) Christian Fellowship in Augusta, Georgia. Thanks for teaching us the Word of God. Dr. Ron and Sue Rockwell, our pastors and spiritual leaders at Harvest Church in Phoenix, Arizona, thanks for being an example of not only teaching, but living a spiritual life. Thanks for teaching us how to love one another the way God wants us to. Special thanks go to apostle John Evans for letting me know it was not my fault, but it was my time. Again, thanks to all our friends. Remember, God loves you, and so do we.

DEDICATION

This book is dedicated to all mankind in hopes that they will return to their first Love and follow His commandments, to love one another as we love ourselves. I hope they will love with a giving love that fills them up each day with joy and happiness, respecting and thinking of others, willing to sacrifice for their neighbors. Remember, "let your speech be always with grace, seasoned with salt, that ye may know how ye ought to answer every man" (Col. 4:6).

CHAPTER 1

THE POWER OF THE TONGUE

The Word of the Lord tells us, "Death and life are in the power of the tongue: and they that love it shall eat the fruit thereof" (Prov. 18:21).

"Those who love to talk will suffer the consequences. Men have died for saying the wrong thing" (Prov. 18:21, TLB).

He that hath an ear, let him hear what the Spirit is saying to him. When we really understand the power of what we say, we can walk and receive all that God has for us. I know you have heard the old saying "Sticks and stones may break my bones, but words will never hurt me." Let me tell you, that is one of the biggest lies you have ever heard. Words are very powerful, and they hurt. And I believe whether it is a positive or negative word, it will stay with you for the rest of your life. (At this moment, you are thinking of something someone said to you or something you said to someone years ago.) No matter what is said, it will have an everlasting effect on the way you live out your life. The words that were spoken to us as kids years ago today have been handed down and are creating death and destruction in the young and old. We are teaching the next generation it is okay to say what they feel. I believe because of a lack of knowledge of the Word of God, people are in rage and anger, which leads to hurtful things being said.

Read what the Word of God tells us:

> Even so the tongue is a small thing, but what enormous damage it can do. A great forest can be set on fire by one tiny spark. And the tongue is a flame of fire. It is full of wickedness, and poisons every part of the body and the tongue is set on fire by hell itself, and can turn our whole lives into a blazing flame of destruction and disaster. Men have trained, or can train, every kind of animal or bird that lives and every kind of reptile and fish, but no human being can tame the tongue. It is always ready to pour out its deadly poison. Sometimes it praises our heavenly Father, and sometimes it breaks out into curses against men who are made like God. And so blessing and cursing come pouring out of the same mouth. Dear brothers, surely this is not right. James 3:5-10, TLB

Note: *As you can see, the tongue can be a blessing and a curse. If you want to use it as a blessing, you* *will need the help of the Holy Spirit. God desires for us to be a blessing to one another, whether it is with money, a helping hand, or kind words or a word of encouragement.*

True Story

Let me tell you a short story of a young man who claimed to be a Christian, who praised God daily, but who got caught up in the language of the world. One day he was at work, and the phone rang. On the line was a female coworker. When he answered, "Hello?" she said, "Booty call." He said, "What?" Then she said, "You have a phone call." Well, that was a seed that the devil planted in his mind. A few days later, he thought he would play the same trick on her that she played on him. He sent her a text message with the title of the message being "Booty call." He went a little further and added that it is just like Lay's potato chips—you can't eat just one; you have to come back for more.

The young lady called him and said she did not like what he had said. The young man apologized to the girl, but the young lady sent the message to her boyfriend, who, in turn, sent it to the girl's father, who was a Marine sergeant major. As you can imagine, that did not go over well with her father. The devil had started a fire, and it began destroying things. The sergeant major went to the young man's boss with a copy of the note. They started an investigation and said the young man was using improper language to employees. Then, he was relieved of his duties.

This is just one example of what the book of James chapter 3 talks about. We must be mindful of the cunning ways of the devil and how he gets you to use the worldly terms that men and women of God should not use. I believe this young man is a Christian just like so many of us.

After reading this book, you will be knowledgeable about the power of the Word and what the Word can do to you and for you. The Word of God tells us His people are destroyed for the lack of knowledge and the rejection of knowledge (Hosea 4:6).

Colossians 4:6 tells us, "Let your speech be always with grace, seasoned with salt, that ye may know how ye ought to answer every man." We, as Christians, are supposed to be the salt of the world, and when we lose it or refuse to get it, we become just like the rest of the world. As the salt, we must add flavor to the situations with which we come in contact. But before we can do this, we must study the Word so we can know it. This is the beginning, letting the Holy Spirit control our speech, because the Word tells us no *man* can tame the tongue. Proverbs 4:7 tells us, "Wisdom is the principal thing; therefore get wisdom: and with all thy getting get understanding."

In my daily walk, I see and hear so many young and old people speaking disgraceful things, having or showing no respect for anyone. I can remember when I was in the world I was the same saying thing not caring who it may hurt. Riding on the bus sitting in a restaurant using language if my grandmother would have heard me she would have knot my teeth out or if one of her friends went back and told her.

Today people are afraid to correct each other and it is affecting the way we raise our children, please take a look around you and tell me what you see and hear. You can't go to a good family movie these days because of the language and the sex scenes, death and destruction will continue because we are taking our kids to these types of movies, and we are speaking the same language in front of them. And we ask why kids are doing what they are doing. It is because this is what we teach them. We learn from our parents, so kids learn from us.

I will repeat what the Bible says in James 3:6: "The tongue is a fire, a world of iniquity: so is the tongue among our members, that it defileth the whole body, and setteth on fire the course of nature; and it is set on fire of hell." We, as Christians, cannot get caught up in the negative and hurtful things of the world. We must be a bright light in a dark alley. We must be the salt of the earth. We have to stop being afraid because fear is of the devil, and it will keep you running from the blessings of the Lord. If you are in this group of people, I am referring to you; you must repent and ask for the Holy Spirit to control what you say. In the book of Psalms, David requests of God, "Create in me a clean heart, O God; and renew a right spirit within me" (51:10).

David said this because he knew something had to change within him, and he could not do it alone. He needed the Holy Spirit, and I believe the Holy Spirit is a warrior. He will give you instructions on how to clean up your act and prepare you for battle. If you did not know you were in a war, this could be the reason you are getting beat up with the things that are coming out of your mouth. "For we are not fighting against people made of flesh and blood, but against persons without bodies, the evil rulers of the unseen world, those mighty satanic beings (thoughts) and great evil princes of darkness who rule this world; and against huge numbers of wicked spirits in the spirit world" (Eph. 6:12, TLB). This is why the Holy Spirit is so important in our lives. When we give the devil victory in the spirit, we act it out in the flesh. We say things we should not, and some of the things we say are not forgettable. On the flip side, some things we hear we don't forget or forgive. Words really do hurt! If they didn't, the Word would not tell us, "Let your speech be always with grace, seasoned with salt, that ye may know how ye ought to answer every man" (Col. 4:6).

Remember, the tongue is unruly, and no man can tame it; you've got to do what David did, and ask for a clean heart. Yes, the heart is where the issues of life come from, and out of the abundance of the heart the mouth speaks. It's the things we don't know about our heart that get us in trouble. Don't misunderstand me; there are good things that come out of the heart, but you've got to put good things in your heart in order for good things to come out of it. This is what the Bible says about the heart: "THE HEART IS DECEITFUL ABOVE ALL THINGS, AND DESPERATELY WICKED: WHO CAN KNOW IT?" (Jer. 17:9, emphasis added). The things we say come from the heart. I believe the things we say have been planted in our hearts from the things we hear, see, and do.

Because we are a negative, revengeful, and angry generation, we kill ourselves by the things we say.

Matthew 12:34-37 tells us:

> O generation of vipers [snakes], how can ye, being evil, speak good things? For out of the abundance of the heart the mouth speaketh. A good man out of the good treasure of the heart bringeth forth good things: and an evil man out of the evil treasure bringeth forth evil things. But I say unto you, that every idle word that men shall speak, they shall give account thereof in the day of judgment. For by thy words thou shalt be justified, and by thy words thou shalt be condemned.

As you can see, the heart controls the tongue, and we know there is life and death in the power of the tongue. Now my questions to you:

1. What do you have in your heart?
2. Who can control your tongue?

CHAPTER 2

LIFE AND DEATH

The Word of God tells us we have a choice and can make decisions about what we want and what we want to do. The book of Joshua talks about such a choice—the covenant renewal with the people that Abraham made with God at Shechem. Joshua 24:15 states, "And if it seem evil unto you to serve the Lord, choose you this day whom ye will serve; whether the gods which your fathers served that were on the other side of the flood, or the gods of the Amorites, in whose land ye dwell: but as for me and my house, we will serve the Lord."

Just as Joshua asked them whom they will serve, I am asking you whom you will serve. There is life and death in your answer.

Whom Will You Serve?

I believe there is a thin line between life and death, and that thin line is not only how we act, but what comes out of our hearts. What we let enter our hearts will come out of our mouths, creating our destiny and forming the actions we implement in life. If you don't believe it, check this out: Everything you know someone spoke to you, or you heard someone say, or you read in a book. Now, there is life and death in what you receive. What we need is a filter system to sift out the death from life. By *death*, I mean both spiritual death and physical death. While we all will die a physical death, we all don't need to die a spiritual death.

Let me expound the two deaths so you understand what I am telling you. Let's start with physical death. Every living being will experience this type of death. This relates to the physical body, the flesh and bones. Make no mistake; this body will cease to function one day. I believe what we have done, have heard, have said, and are saying determine the physical movement of our bodies. Remember, death came to man because of what one man *did*; you can read the story in Genesis chapter 3, on the Fall of man.

Now let me explain spiritual death—simply being separated from God. This is the type of death you do not want. When you are not living according to the Word of God, you are spiritually dead. John 5:24 tells us, "Verily, Verily, I say unto you, He that heareth my word, and believeth on him that sent me, hath everlasting life, and shall not come into condemnation; but is passed from death unto life." This tells me we must believe and not have doubt in our hearts. When we begin to have doubt in our hearts, we start speaking it with our mouths, and when we start doing that, we begin killing our spirit. Don't forget what Proverbs 18:21 says: "The tongue has the power of life and death, and those who love it will eat its fruit" (NIV).

We must really be careful what we say and what we let into our hearts. After all, our lives depend on what we say. Also, we must teach our children to say the right things, as Proverbs 22:6 says: "Train up a child in the way he should go: and when he is old, he will not depart from it." Stop and think about what you hear daily from our young children. They didn't just come up with some of the things you hear them say on their own. On the contrary, these things came from us! We are teaching this, or should I say, we are killing them spiritually by being so negative in our words. Proverbs 12:18-20 tells us:

> There is that speaketh like the piercings of a sword: but the tongue of the wise is health. The lip of truth shall be established for ever: but a lying tongue is but for a moment. Deceit is in the heart of them that imagine evil: but to the counsellors of peace is joy.

We must remember, it is not what goes into our mouths that defiles us; rather, it is what comes *out* of our mouths. Life and death are in the power of the tongue. Most of us are alive in the flesh, but dead in the Spirit. With these people, the devil controls the flesh, and as long as he controls it, we will be dead to Christ. I am a living testimony of Proverbs 22:6: "Train up a child in the way he should go: and when he is old, he will not depart from it." I thank my grandmother who never said a negative word to me about life. When I was a young boy, she drilled two things into my heart, and they were work and go to church. When I look back over my life, I realize when I was still young, I was working, and I have never stopped. Now I see why she wanted me to work. If I work, I can give to God my firstfruits, and He will take care of me and give me the things I desire. I thank her for instilling that in my heart.

The part about going to church stayed in my heart; I never stopped going to church, even when I was doing sinful things. In 1981, when my family and I were on our way to Ohio to visit my in-laws, I had been driving for a few hours when I got tired. So we pulled into a rest stop for a few hours, and then we got back on the road at about 3 A.M. My wife and daughter were still asleep, and I decided to smoke a joint. After about an hour, I started to feel sleepy. My eyes felt very heavy. Despite this, I continued to drive. I fell asleep, and the car drifted to my left and hit the shoulder of the road. I panicked. I hit the gas instead of the brakes and went into a small ditch. The car flipped over and landed on its top, then slid down the highway, meeting oncoming traffic. The front windshield was gone. Sparks were flying, and lights were coming at us. It was an eighteen-wheeler. I know God gave him the eyes to see our car from a distance. He slowed down about fifty yards from us, pulled over to the side, jumped out, and ran over to help us. By the grace of God, the only injury we got was my wife had a small cut on her knee. I thank God for saving our lives. I kept going to church and reading my Bible once in a while, still not fully understanding what was happening to me.

One time, I got an assignment to go to Germany. I went first to get things set up and then sent for my family. It always happens when you go somewhere and you are living in the flesh that you will find someone else who lives in the flesh, or they will find you, so it will become a death walk all over again. I started drinking and smoking with the guys and still going to church on Sundays and sometimes on Wednesday nights. I thank God for my wife, who is a praying woman. The first week my family arrived, I wanted to introduce her to everyone, so I threw a homecoming party. I was drinking all day. At about midnight, everyone started to leave. A few people said they were going to the pub down the street, so I said I was going too. My wife tried to tell me not to go, but trying to tell a drunk person not to do something doesn't work — at least it did not work with me that night. I could have walked to the pub; it was only two blocks from our apartment. But I wanted to drive, so I got in my car, went to the pub, and stayed until 3 A.M., drinking the whole time, so much that everything was looking gray. My friend did not have a ride home, so I said, "Come on, I will take you home." I took him home, and we talked for about thirty minutes. He got out of the car and went to his apartment, while I started back home. It was about 4:30 A.M. when, as I was driving, I hit a bump in the road and my music tapes dropped on the floor. While still driving, I bent over to pick them up. When I leaned over, I turned the wheel. When I got back up, I noticed I was headed straight for an apple tree. I turned the wheel quickly to the left and went over the side, dropping about twenty-five feet, and then hit another apple tree head-on.

After the wreck, the car was in a V shape. It just so happened that someone was passing by, saw what had happened, stopped, and helped me. Again, I was saved by the grace of God. The only injury I sustained was a scratch on my shoulder. Now, going home was the toughest thing I had to do. I had to tell my wife I totaled the car after she begged me not to go because I was too drunk. I did not tell her when I got home. Instead, I slept on the sofa, and later that day, I broke the news to her. Needless to say, she was not happy. I was still going to church and reading my Bible from time to time. This is what happened to me when I was walking the death walk, being led by the flesh, because of words I had spoken years earlier.

In the movie "The Green Mile," there is a saying, "DEAD MAN WALKING." Brothers and sisters, that was me, a dead man walking. Now I know why my grandmother prayed for me and wanted me always to go to church. God had a plan for my life. He gave me new friends. He gave me a new life. I was moved from darkness to light, and He is using me to tell men He has a better life for them if they just trust Him. Listen to the men and women He has placed in your path who are teaching you the true Word of God.

When you bring the flesh under control, turning away from those things that so easily beset you, then and only then will you begin to really live. You also must activate the Holy Spirit, pray for it to come in and upon you, because you will need Him to keep you from falling back into your old habits and becoming a "dead man walking." When you begin to live for God, this is what will intensify, and you will need to know this: "For you are not fighting against people made of flesh and blood, but against persons without bodies, the evil rulers of the unseen world, those mighty satanic beings and great evil princes of darkness who rule this world; and against huge numbers of wicked spirits in the spirit world. So use every piece of God's armor to resist the enemy whenever he attacks, and when it is all over, you will still be standing up" (Eph. 6:12-13, TLB). When you become spiritually alive, you will be at peace with God, yourself, family, friends, and your neighbors. I am not saying you will no longer be confronted with the things you used to do; I am saying when you turn them over to God and you stand on His Word, you will overcome any temptation with which you are confronted.

> ***Note:*** *This is what the Word of God is saying to you: "There hath no temptation taken you but such as is common to man: but God is faithful, who will not suffer you to be tempted above that ye are able; but will with the temptation also make a way to escape, that ye may be able to bear it" (1 Cor. 10:13).*

Please understand, things that happen to you come from what you say or what you said or what you let into your heart and believed. As Proverbs 18:21 tells us, "Death and life are in the power of the tongue: and they that love it shall eat the fruit thereof."

I will be referring to this Scripture throughout this book to make you aware that what you say can kill you or save your life. Please don't misunderstand me; everyone will die a physical death one day. I am not talking about that natural death. I am talking about spiritual death. Everyone will not die a spiritual death, and I want you to be in the number that will *not die a spiritual death*.

Are you speaking life or death?

CHAPTER 3

THE THINGS WE SAY

I believe life is a duplication. What do I mean by that? Well, take a look around you. What do you see and hear? How many of the things that we see and hear do we repeat, even if not realizing what we are saying sometimes? There is nothing new that you say or hear. Here is the thing about what we hear: It affects what we do in life and what we say to one another, all because it gets in our hearts. We listen to those filthy rap CDs, watch those outrageous movies, and even let our children listen to and watch them. And we wonder why our kids don't respect us. These things get in our hearts, and our minds begin to act on what our hearts have stored in them. Matthew 15:19 says, "For out of the HEART proceed evil thoughts, murders, adulteries, fornications, thefts, false witness, blasphemies" (emphasis added). This is all because we let these things get in, and we act them out.

Let us tackle each one of these:

Murders—Look around you at the needless killing that is happening these days. Each day it's getting worse. When we talk about murder, we are not only talking about a physical death, but a spiritual death also. We all have murdered someone, or someone has murdered us. What do I mean? Have you ever had someone tell you, you will never amount to anything, you are a loser, you are fat, you are ugly, you can't do anything right, you are a dummy, you are stupid, you are a little tramp, there is no God? If no one said any of these things to you, you may have said at least one of them to someone or heard someone say them. You may have even thought about telling someone something like that. Well, this is what the Word tells us in Proverbs 23:7: "For as he thinketh in his HEART, so is he" (emphasis added).

Adulteries—What you say or what you receive can lead to a lifestyle of adulteries. Look at some of the people in Hollywood or pro athletes. Look in your own neighborhood, even in the church. I know you know someone who is weak in this area, maybe even you. The TV and movies are not helping, so what we need to do is stop watching the types of things that lead us in this sinful, destructive lifestyle. Remember, "as he thinketh in his heart, so is he." I believe we can speak life into our family, friends, and neighbors when we see or hear these things happening.

Fornications—What is this? It is sexual intercourse between a man and a woman not married to each other. I know this hit home with a lot of people, and everyone is doing it. That type of thinking has gotten a lot of us in trouble. We showed it to our children, and they think it is something that should happen at an early age. I don't have to tell what it has done; just look around. So many of us are putting our thoughts in action, and many others are thinking about what it would be like if they could have someone else. However, that is just as bad as taking action physically. Remember, "as he thinketh in his heart, so is he."

Thefts — While some people work hard to get what they have, others say, "Let us take what they have. They don't need it; they have more than enough. Steal it from them. It is easy." They don't realize it will hurt the whole community because those people will be living in fear. Everything you can name is being taken from someone who has more. Why? We say they won't miss it or they have enough. But it is not about whether they will miss it; it's about living a righteous life, putting your trust in God and not yielding to the ways of the devil. It is not for us to say who has enough and who doesn't. It is not our right to take from others.

Is stealing something we tell or show our children? I would hope not, but we must face reality. This is what is going on today, and we are saying it is the economy. There are jobs out there, but people don't want them because they are full of pride, and the jobs are low-paying. Well, if my family needed to eat or my rent needed to be paid, I better get two of those low-paying jobs and not steal from others. You may get away from man, but you will *not* get away from

God. Not only do the things we say influence those around us, but the way we act also sends a message to the people around us. Our action adds fuel to the fire of our tongue. Stealing is not right. This is hard love, but the Word tells us this: "For even when we were with you, this we commanded you, that if any would not work, neither should he eat" (2 Thess. 3:10). Remember the Ten Commandments, which God gave to Moses. The eighth commandment is "Thou shalt not steal" (Exod. 20:15). You can read about all of them in Exodus chapter 20.

Note: The Ten Commandments were written on a tablet and given to Moses. When Christ came on the scene and we accepted Him, the commandments were written on the tables of our hearts.

False witness — Here, we are still talking about the things we say. The bottom line: Bearing false witness is telling a lie. This is something that has hit home with everyone at some point in his or her life. Some of us are still doing it. Some of us have done it so long that it is second nature. The sad thing is when we do it, we say things around our children, and they pick up on it and take it to another level. Keep in mind, the things we say and the people we hang out with determine our destiny. First Corinthians 15:33-34 (RSV) tells us: "Do not be deceived: 'Bad company ruins good morals.' Come to your right mind, and sin no more. For some have no knowledge of God. I say this to your shame." Another version of this Scripture passage, from the

NIV, says it like this: "Do not be misled: 'Bad company corrupts good character.' Come back to your senses as you ought, and stop sinning; for there are some who are ignorant of God—I say this to your shame." You see, we must be careful about whom we hang out with because the things they do and say will get into our hearts if we are not strong enough to fight them off, and before we know it, we are bearing false witness about or to someone.

Psalm 101:7-8 (TLB) states: "But I will not allow those who deceive and lie to stay in my house. My daily task will be to ferret out criminals and free the city of God from their grip." As you can see, it is not good to be a liar. There is life and death in the power of the tongue. The ball is in your court; you must choose. To get a better idea of some of the things we say, please see the following list. Also see what God says about what we say.

1. We say:
I don't have anything.

God says:
"Ask and you will receive" (John 16:24, NIV).

2. We say:
It is impossible.

God says:
All things are possible (Luke 18:27).

3. We say:

Whom can I trust?

God says:
"Trust in the Lord" (Ps. 37:3).

4. We say:
I am tired.

God says:
"I will give you rest" (Matt. 11:28).

5. We say:
I don't want to hear that.

God says:
My son, pay attention (Prov. 4:20-22).

6. We say:
Nobody loves me.

God says:
I love you (John 3:16).

7. We say:
I can't make it.

God says:
"My grace is sufficient" (2 Cor. 12:9).

8. We say:
I can't figure things out.

God says:
I will direct your paths (Prov. 3:5-6).

9. We say:
I can't do it.

God says:
You can do all things (Phil. 4:13).

10. We say:
I am not able.

God says:
I am able (2 Cor. 9:8).

11. We say:
I am all alone.

God says:
I will never leave you (Heb. 13:5).

12. We say:
It's not working.

God says:
"All things work together" (Rom. 8:28).

13. We say:
I am not smart enough.

God says:
I will give you wisdom (1 Cor. 1:30).

14. We say:
I can't forgive myself.

God says:
I forgive you (1 John 1:9).

15. We say:
I have nothing.

God says:
I will supply your needs (Phil. 4:19).

16. We say:
I don't know.

God says:
"Study to shew thyself" (2 Tim. 2:15).

17. We say:
I am afraid.

God says:
I have not given you the spirit of fear (2 Tim. 1:7).

18. We say:
I don't believe it.

God says:
"My people are destroyed for lack of knowledge" (Hosea 4:6).

19. We say:
I am always worried.

God says:
Cast all your cares on me (1 Pet. 5:7).

20. We say:
I hate them.

God says:
"Love your enemies" (Matt. 5:44).

These are some of the many things we say every day that are very negative, and they keep us from reaching our full potential in Christ. Not only are they keeping us from reaching our full potential, but they are also hurting everyone around us. When we are not careful about what we say and do, it affects not only us, but everyone who means anything to us. It is like the domino effect—it does not stop until everyone feels the effect of what we said or did. Remember, it is not only what you say that affects others; actions also speak very loudly.

Do not misunderstand me. At times, good things are said, but they are few and far between. We live in a world that loves negative and hurtful things. Just look at the political world, the new media, and Hollywood—they thrive on negative and hurtful things. And we, as people of this society, love to hear and see negative things. Even we Christians are right in the middle of all the gossip. This is how those people make their money, and we all know the Word tells us "the love of money is the root of all evil" (1 Tim. 6:10). People will say or do anything for the dollar. The things we say sometimes really make us question whether we are real Christians or faking it.

I have been in men's Bible studies where men try to turn the study into a political forum because they don't like the president. We, as Christians, should know better and not talk about people. There is life and death in the power of the tongue. The things we say not only hurt the people we are talking to or about. These things also affect the person who is doing the talking. Remember, God wants us to pray for one another, speaking life—not death—to our fellow man.

Check out what Proverbs 18:6-8 says: "A fool's lips enter into contention, and his mouth calleth for strokes. A fool's mouth is his DESTRUCTION, and his lips are the snare of his soul. The words of a talebearer are as wounds, and they go down into the innermost parts of the belly." Again, you can see there is power in what you say. Your words can give you life, or they can give you death. Which do you choose? Remember what Hosea 4:6 says: "My people are destroyed for lack of knowledge: because thou hast rejected knowledge, I will also reject thee, that thou shalt be no priest to me: seeing thou hast forgotten the law of thy God, I will also forget thy children." Please read that verse again. What you say is affecting your children, and trust me, what they learn at home they will show when they go away from home.

When you hear a young child cursing, he or she has learned it from an adult. When you see a young kid steal from a person or store, it's because he or she saw someone else do it. When you see a young kid shooting someone, it's because the child saw someone else, likely another adult, do that. And remember, when you see your young daughters getting pregnant, they saw or heard someone having sex. What we need to say to them, we don't; we feel ashamed to say it. The things we need to be talking about we aren't, and in this case, we are killing our kids. We need to teach them the Word of God. The Word tells us to train our children in the way they should go, and when they are old, they will not depart from it. We can talk about anything with our children but sex and the Bible because we don't want to use those words around them. We are not speaking to them verbally; we are speaking death to them mentally. Their minds are dead to the righteous things of God. I know you are wondering, *What are the righteous things of God that we are to teach them?* If you have to ask that question, you need to be taught the Word also.

Let us start in Deuteronomy 6:5-9:

Thou shalt love the Lord thy God with all thine heart, and with all thy soul.

V. 5

Note: *This is the first thing you teach your children; this is teaching them life.*

And these words, which I command thee this day, shall be in thine heart.

V. 6

Note: *We have been commanded to teach them the love of God. Why can't we follow what we have been told? The words are in our hearts.*

And thou shalt teach them diligently unto thy children, and shalt talk of them when thou sittest in thine house, and when thou walkest by the way, and when thou liest down, and when thou risest up.

V. 7

Note: *I know why we are not teaching our children when we are in the house. Please tell me if I am wrong. We are on the computer, we are cooking and don't have time, we are watching sports on TV, we are on the cell phone with a friend, we let them play the Xbox, we let them play outside, we let them go to their friend's house, or we let them play on the computer for a while. These are some of the excuses we use. Please stop killing your children. Teach them the Word of God; the time is at hand.*

And thou shalt bind them for a sign upon thine hand, and they shall be as frontlets between thine eyes.

V. 8

Note: *We are to teach them so the Word will be in front of them at all times, so they know what and when to speak, and when they do, it will be to edify someone and not to plant death to them.*

And thou shalt write them upon the posts of thy house, and on thy gates.

V. 9

Notes: *We must speak positive words—the Word of God—in our house all the time, and place them on the doors to our bedrooms, living room, den, family room, kitchen, and bathrooms. When we don't do that, things begin to happen. We begin to let lying spirits in our home, and they get in through what we say, what we watch, and what we hear. The devil is very cunning. His primary mission is to seek, kill, and destroy, and he will use any means to accomplish his mission. Brothers and sisters, we must stop yielding to his devices. They are killing us because we lack the knowledge and reject the knowledge. Wake up, and see there is life and death in the power of the tongue!*

What language are you speaking?
Is it life or death?_____

CHAPTER 4

THE THINGS PEOPLE SAY TO US

We are living our lives according to what the world tells us. The sad thing about that is we are not looking at or listening to the things that will give us eternal life. We are living for the moment and not keeping the end in mind. What I mean is we are living like there is no afterlife, all because the devil has blinded the eyes of man so the devil may recruit him in his army. This all began when we were young. Someone may have told you that you will never be anything. You keep that thought in the back of your mind, and the devil plays on that thought. He puts things in front of you that bring that thought to mind, and you play it out, and before you know it, you have done something wrong. This gives power to your thoughts creating nothing, just like you were told when you were young that you would never be anything and you were no good.

Well, this is what God says about that: "But ye are a chosen generation, a royal priesthood, an holy nation, a peculiar people; that ye should shew forth the praises of him who hath called you out of darkness into his marvellous light" (1 Pet. 2:9).

We really need to listen to what God's Word is telling us and not what the TV, movies, radio, and our unsaved loved ones and friends are saying.

Your parents, your friends, your teacher, or a family member may have told you that you were stupid or crazy. Let me tell you that you are not stupid. You are not crazy. Instead, you are the joy of our Lord and Savior, Jesus Christ. When you acknowledge Him, this is what God says to His family, and you are in His family: "The steps of a good man are ordered by the LORD: and he delighteth in his way" (Ps. 37:23). When we listen to the words of God, they bring joy, peace, and life to our spiritual being, and we live them out in a fleshly body. People may call you names and may say bad things about you, but if you stay focused on Him, you will be strong in the power of His might. Please listen to these words, and sin not with your tongue. You should keep your mouth bridled while the wicked is before you (Ps. 39:1). "Vengeance is mine," said the Lord. Know you can fight the devil in the spirit realm because of the things people say to you and about you. O the things we say about others too. Yes, we say bad things about others, even our friends.

Short Story

When I was very young, all the boys teased me, and the girls laughed at me because of my clothes. I had patches on my jeans where my grandmother had fixed the holes. Some of them she did not fix, so I went to school with holes in my jeans. My shoes had holes in them. Kids would run through the water and laugh at me because I could not do that because of the holes in the bottoms of my shoes. My nickname was "Patches" because of how I looked.

As a young kid in third, fourth, and fifth grades, it was no fun going to school. I did not know God the way I do now. Yes, I went to church because in my grandmother's house, that is what you did. I am telling you this because you may not know how much words do hurt, and that you can overcome that hurt through God's love. I forgave those who teased me back then. No, I did not forget, but I promised myself that when I grew up and could buy my own clothes, I would never wear clothes with holes in them again.

God blessed me with a grandmother who kept me focused on working and going to church. During that time, going to school was no fun because I had to listen to what people were saying about me. When I look back at things that they said about me, I see I turned it around to give me strength and motivation to have the best things in life. It is amazing how things have changed. I was ashamed to wear clothes with holes in them and was teased and called hurtful names because I did. Now look at what people are wearing—jeans with holes, even holes where there should not be holes. They are paying big money for these clothes. Today kids think you are cool if you wear them. In my time, kids thought you were poor. I said this to let you know you control your own destiny. We must stop giving ear to the negative things people say to us and about us. Most of all, we must forgive them for their ignorance, and pray for them.

Note: *And when ye stand praying, forgive, if ye have ought against any: that your Father also which is in heaven may forgive you your trespasses. But if ye do not forgive, neither will your Father which is in heaven forgive your trespasses (Mark 11:25-26).*

Following are a couple of examples of negative things people say.

1. *"God is not real."* Well, let me tell you, my God says: "My people are destroyed . . . because thou hast rejected knowledge, I will also reject thee, that thou shalt be no priest to me: seeing thou hast forgotten the law of thy God, I will also forget thy children" (Hosea 4:6). Everything we do or say has an effect on our children. We must really study the Word of God to know we must love Him first and then love our neighbors.

2. *"I don't see what you see in him anyway. He will never amount to anything."* Have you heard this before? Well, God says this: "Study to shew thyself approved unto God, a workman that needeth not to be ashamed, rightly dividing the word of truth" (2 Tim. 2:15). "I can do all things through Christ which strengtheneth me" (Phil. 4:13). We must turn the negative into positive just like the Word of God tells us. Something to remember: The devil's works in the

negative, creating thoughts and ideas for people to work out in the flesh, only come true when we pay attention to them. Just stop and think for a moment. Ninety percent of the things you hear are negative—even your conversations are negative. Why is that? Well, most of us were never in a positive environment of family and friends. Therefore, trying to learn to be positive will take your seeking "the kingdom of God, and his righteousness; and all these things shall be added unto you" (Matt. 6:33).

Let me tell you three principal laws that will never change, and once you understand them, you will be able to discern the things you say and hear. "While the earth remaineth, seedtime and harvest, and cold and heat, and summer and winter, and day and night shall not CEASE" (Gen. 8:22, emphasis added). Let me break this down a little more for you. As long as the earth is here, there will be seedtime and harvest, meaning if you plant something, there will come a time to harvest what was planted. There will always be cold and heat, summer and winter, and night and day. All of this will always be, as long as there is the earth. This was set in play by the Creator Himself and cannot be broken or changed by man.

Let us talk a little bit about the seedtime and harvest. I would say everything that is happening to you is from a seed you or someone else planted sometime during your life. Now these things are beginning to spring up, and you are wondering why. It is because of what you did or said, or what someone else did or said. It is what we call seedtime and harvest. Remember when you said, "I am catching a cold"? Nine times out of ten, you got the cold. Remember when you said, "I am getting sick"? Remember when you said, "I am getting a headache"? Remember when you said, "He is cheating on me"? Remember when you said, "I am broke"? Remember when you said, "I will be the next one laid off"? Remember when you said, "I am not going to pass this test"? Remember when you said, "My car is not going to start"? Remember when you said, "My kids are getting the flu"? I could go on and on about the negative seeds we plant every day. And when they germinate and come to pass, it starts affecting our lives. We ask, "Why me, Lord?" Now you don't have to ask, "Why me, Lord?" anymore. I am telling you why: You are planting negative seeds in your life, and your family members' and friends' lives. I believe if we keep our minds on God and remain full of faith, we can take note from Abraham.

In the book of Romans, read what Paul said about Abraham:

(As it is written, I HAVE MADE THEE A FATHER OF MANY NATIONS,) *[Note: This means if we follow the faith of Abraham, we will get what we ask for.]* before him whom he believed, even God, who quickeneth the dead [who make the dead alive again], and calleth those things which be not as though they were. *[Note: We need to speak life into our situations by claiming the things we want but don't have yet as though we have them, and doing it with faith.]* Who against hope believed in hope, that he might become the father of many nations, according to that which was spoken, So SHALL THY SEED BE. *[Note: Here the odds were against Abraham, but he kept the faith, and he spoke life into what was promised to him.]* And being not weak in faith, he considered not his own body now dead, when he was about an hundred years old, neither yet the deadness of Sarah's womb: He staggered not at the promise of God through unbelief; but was strong in faith, giving glory to God; and being fully persuaded that, what he had promised, he was able also to perform.

Romans 4:17-21

Note: There is life and death in the power of the tongue. There are two types of death: spiritual, where you are separated from God, and physical, where you have stopped breathing. You have power over both of them through what you say. Keep in mind, what we say comes from the heart. "For as he thinketh in his heart, so is he: Eat and drink, saith he to thee; but his heart is not with thee" (Proverbs 23:7).

My question to you is, where is your heart, and what is it telling your tongue to speak? To clean up what you are saying, pray to God, "Create in me a clean heart, O God; and renew a right spirit within me" (Ps. 50:10). So many lives have been destroyed because we can't control our tongues, which is an unruly body part. The devil is very tricky, for he knows the way to your heart is through your eyes. He will get you to admire something, and when that happens, he puts desire in your heart. When desire gets in the heart, it creates an acquiring spirit in the heart. When this happens, you are going to get what you desire, or you are going to say it, no matter whom it hurts, as long as you get what you admire. This is where things get deadly if you are saying and doing the wrong things.

When you are standing on the Word of God, you will get slammed with all kinds of things, for it is written that we will be persecuted for his name's sake. On the other hand, we must let our speech "be always with grace, seasoned with salt, that ye may know how ye ought to answer every man" (Col. 4:6). We have Christians saying bad things about one another, even bad things about the pastor, not realizing the damage the things said are doing. We are to be in the world, but not *of* the world. We are born again into the kingdom of our Lord and Savior, Jesus Christ. We are to help and pray for one another.

Bible nugget: *"The tongue is a fire, a world of iniquity: so is the tongue among our members [other body parts], that it defileth the whole body, and setteth on fire the course of nature; and it is set on fire of hell" (James 3:6).*

As I have stated, there is life and death in the power of the tongue. No man can tame it; it is unruly, evil, and full of deadly poison. Take a look around you, read the newspaper, listen to the media, and listen to conversations at work, in your bridge club, and in your group of soccer moms. We are a gossiping society that needs to convert all the gossip into prayers for ourselves and others who are gossiping. In many cases, we are not the ones who are gossiping, but we are encouraging the gossip because we are listening to it, not knowing the Word tells us, "BE NOT DECEIVED: EVIL COMMUNICATIONS CORRUPT GOOD MANNERS" (1 Cor. 15:33, emphasis added).

We Christians must watch what we say and what we do all the time because the devil has his soldiers watching us every day and night. Let me tell you a short story about something that happened to me a few years ago.

I manage a fitness center for the Air Force, and when you are the boss, a lot of your staff members don't like some of the things you say or do. For instance, a few were out to get me because I let them know I believe in Jesus Christ. I don't smoke, I don't drink, and I don't curse, and from time to time, I would talk to the men and try to get them to stop doing some of the things they were doing, saying to come to church with me. I found out later there are two things you don't talk about in the workplace: religion and politics. One morning, we were setting up for a 5K fun run, and before we left the fitness center, one of the employees said to me she did not believe in Jesus Christ because He was not real. This young lady was of the Jewish faith. I told her He is real, and it was the Jews who crucified Him. The conversation continued after the run was finished, about how He died. I said something, or all the things I was saying hit at once, and she started crying and ran away from where we were. I called to her and apologized if I said something that offended her.

Then, I thought this was the last of the situation. But when we got back to the fitness center, I found out my assistant took her to the commanders' office to report me for talking about religion at work and insulting one of the employees. The commanders came to my office and asked me what had happened. I explained, and he understood, and told me not to speak about religion at work. I called the young lady and my assistant to my office and apologized to her. She accepted my apology, and the matter was finished . . . or so I thought.

Note: *We really need to watch what we say and obey the ones who are over us. This is what God wants us to do. But don't be afraid to speak up about God, for He will protect you from your enemies.*

A few months passed, and we were in the process of purchasing new uniforms for all employees. There was a problem with the female pants; the women complained the seat of the pants was too long. They said it made them feel like they did not have any butt. We ordered the pants from another company, and one day I went into the back office, where three or four employees were sitting. One of the female employees had tried on the new pants, and they wanted me to look at them on her and let them know how they fit. The young lady stood in front of me and turned to the side. I said to turn around so I could see the butt, and she did so. I asked how they felt, and she said okay. I said okay too. I thought that was the last of it about the pants.

Note: *Again, it is how you say what you are saying because everyone doesn't receive and think about things the same way. As I found out later, what you mean is sometimes not what they receive, and this could create something negative, depending on how you say it. Remember, the tongue is unruly, and it speaks what is in the heart.*

One day I told the same young lady who had the pants on when I inspected them on her to make an announcement over the intercom. She told me she was not going to do it, and I told her yes, she was going to do it. She said she would quit first, so I said okay. I completed the paperwork to give her a letter of reprimand for disobeying a direct order. She refused to sign the letter, and she quit. Then she wrote a letter to the commanding general, filing a sexual harassment charge against me for making her feel uncomfortable when I said to turn and let me see the butt area of the pants. (Now, this was the area of the pants that all the females were complaining was too saggy, and they did not like it.) After that, an investigation started about the things I said in the past that people did not like. This was their time to sock it to me. Among the things they (two of my female supervisors whom I trusted) wrote in a statement to the investigator was that I talked about the Bible (religion) too much, and they didn't like it.

One day all the guys were standing around, talking about the younger generation, how they don't have any respect and about the unwise things they do to get in trouble. My response to what we were talking about was most of the kids came from single-parent families, with only the mother as a parent, and didn't have a good spiritual foundation teaching them the Word of God. At that moment, the two female employees came up to hear what we were talking about.

When they heard what I was saying, they walked away. Later, they brought this up to the investigator, putting it in their statements. I am not saying I used the correct words when I told the young lady to turn and let me see the butt area—everyone else except one person had a problem with what I said, and I would agree with them. But when I said what I said, it was using the term they used. I learned two things from this experience:

1. Choose your words carefully before you speak, and know to whom you are talking.
2. Don't ever be afraid to speak about what the Word of God says; just know *how* to say it.

Remember, Satan has blinded the eyes and deafened the ears of unbelievers, so that they only hear what he is saying to them, and that is to destroy the men and women of God through lies and deceit.

At this point, my two questions for you are:

1. What are you saying?
2. What are you doing about it?

Notes: *"The tongue of the wise useth knowledge aright: but the mouth of fools poureth out foolishness" (Prov. 15:2). "The heart of him that hath understanding seeketh knowledge: but the mouth of fools feedeth on foolishness" (Prov. 15:14).*

My point in all of this is we, as men and women of God, need to set a better example for both believers and unbelievers. We really need to watch what we say, when we say it, and how we say it. We are the salt of the world. If we lose our salt, we will be just like the rest of the world—lost without respect for others. I truly believe the things all of us say come from the heart because the Word of God tells us the issues of life come from the heart. That also tells me if they are coming out of the heart, they had to be put in there. Now ask yourself, *If it's there, where did I get it from?* I'll tell you where it came from; it came from the company we keep, the things we see, the things we listen to, and the teaching we receive from others. Now you see how important it is to put good things in your heart. Heed what Colossians 4:6 says: "Let your speech be always with grace, seasoned with salt, that ye may know how ye ought to answer every man."

CHAPTER 5

THE FORCES OF GOOD VS. THE FORCES OF EVIL

We all know there are two sides to every story or situation. Well, it is the same in the physical and spiritual world. For every good thing God has said about man, Satan has said bad things or created a way for the bad things to show their ugly heads in man. There are so many examples. I can even give you a few, and you have some of your own as well.

Look at what is happening with the bullying of kids in school. Kids are being called hurtful names, pushed, and spit on, and it hurts, even leading to their death. I don't blame the kids for saying what they say or doing what they do; the blame falls on us, as parents, because we are not doing what we were commanded to do. What are we supposed to do? I am glad you asked that question. Let us go to the force of good instruction. Deuteronomy 6:5-7 says:

"And thou shalt love the LORD thy God with all thine heart, and with all thy soul, and with all thy might. And these words, which I command thee this day, shall be in thine HEART: And thou shalt TEACH them diligently unto thy CHILDREN, and shalt talk of them when thou sittest in thine house, and when thou walkest by the way, and when thou liest down, and when thou risest up" (emphasis added).

As you can see, we must start at home with our children. When they are young, we must instill the spirit of love and the spirit of compassion, teaching them that what we say does matter, and it has a lifelong effect on others. The forces of evil would have you think words don't matter, and if they do, so what; if you were wronged, you've got to pay the person back or hurt him for hurting you. Kids are losing their lives over words that we taught or are teaching our kids. This evil force must be stopped! We must go back to our first love. We must ask for strength to fight these vile forces. There are three ways to fight the battle with the forces of evil: through the power of prayer, through faith in fasting, and by teaching our children the Word of God.

I know in today's society, it is not cool to speak of God. You can get in trouble. This is another tactic that the devil uses to discourage children of God (forces of good). Those in the world can talk about anything they want and not get any backlash from what is said. This is another sign the forces of evil control this world system, leading the ones who are following him to destruction. Brothers and sisters, the Antichrist is already here, hard at work with all of us.

Note: Before we can teach others God's Word, we must know it ourselves. That means we need to study the Word, just as 2 Timothy 2:15 says: "Study to shew thyself approved unto God, a workman that needeth not to be ashamed, rightly dividing the word of truth." Then we can come to the realization that negative words and actions really have a lasting effect on the way we live our lives. Yes, negative actions can hurt also; you don't have to speak to hurt someone. The way you treat people also matters, and the forces of evil know that. The devil will deal with you in the spirit realm, causing you to act out that thought of hate or dislike.

Look back at your life. I am willing to say you have or had someone in your life you have not spoken to in months or even years. My question to you is, why? Was it something the person said or did to you, or did you do something to that person? This is the work of evil forces working in the spirit realm, creating and developing issues in the HEART because the devil knows out of the heart come the issues of life. We say evil and nasty things to people because we are a negative, vengeful, and prideful generation. Let me explain. We always think of the negative things, no matter how much positive we do or people do for us. We will always find the negative to talk about; these are tactics of evil forces. We are vengeful if someone does something to us. We think such things as, *I will get them back! I am not going to take that! You don't mess with me! They don't know whom they are dealing with!* Does this sound like someone you know? This is what I have learned, and I want you to know that you can do it too: "But I say unto you, LOVE your enemies, bless them that curse you, do good to them that hate you, and pray for them which despitefully use you, and persecute you" (Matt. 5:44, emphasis added).

Now, let me tell you, this is not an easy thing to do. It will take every bit of faith and trust in God that His Word is true when He said vengeance belongs to Him (Deut. 32:35). The next thing we have is negative pride—being too prideful to say, "I am sorry for saying those things to you." This is the leading cause of our not speaking to friends, family, and neighbors. Pride is one of the three forces of evil that the devil uses to recruit soldiers in his army. First John 2:16 says: "For all that is in the world, the lust of the flesh, and the lust of the eyes, and the pride of life, is not of the Father, but is of the world." When we possess these three things, we will say or do anything to hurt someone.

I was told a story about Jesus and Satan. They were given a computer test, during which they had to type two pages of information on the computer. They were given a certain amount of time to finish the test. Just as the judge said time was up, the power went out. When the judge went to check Satan's computer, the judge could not find anything that he had typed. When the judge checked Jesus' computer, everything He typed was there. Satan asked, "How did that happen?" In reply, Jesus said, "I SAVE." The truth to this story is you don't have anything with Satan except spiritual death. But with Jesus, when you choose to side with the good forces, you have eternal life.

So many of us have sold our souls to the devil just to have material things, just to have status in the church and in the community, without knowing the things we do and say we will be held accountable for. There is another principle we fail to understand, or we don't know. Genesis 8:22 tells us this: "While the earth remaineth, SEEDTIME and HARVEST, and cold and heat, and summer and winter, and day and night shall not cease" (emphasis added). I know you are asking yourself, *What is he saying?* I am glad you asked that question. What I want to bring out of this Scripture is seedtime and harvest. I believe you already understand hot and cold, and day and night. I don't think you understand seedtime and harvest, but after reading this book, you will have a better understanding of the verse, along with the things you say and do that are evil and good.

Let me break it down for you in a simple way. Let us use a farmer, for example. A farmer plants his seed. He puts it in the ground and waters it, and it begins to germinate in the ground. After a while, a small bud pops up out of the ground. And after weeks or months, it is harvest time. The fruits of his labor are finally coming to reality. He is now ready to reap what he sowed. The words we speak and the words we let into our hearts have that same farmer effect. They will germinate and grow in our hearts, and they will come out of our mouths because they are in our hearts. When we are raised in a negative environment (one with evil forces), they will remain there throughout

THE FORCES OF GOOD VS. THE FORCES OF EVIL

our adult life, unless we are taught that the things we say will come to pass. Whether they are good or bad, they will come to pass because that is a principle of God, and His Word is for all. But the devil will try and change it for his benefit to create sadness and death. I am talking about physical and spiritual death.

The Father wants us to speak positively all the time, no matter what the situation looks like. He said to call those things that are not as though they were. This means though you may not have them now, speak like you have them, not only to yourself, but to others. A good example of this is found in the Bible, with the story of Abraham, when he was told he would be the father of many nations. You can read about it in the book of Romans chapter 4. Remember, being positive through the forces of good is always victorious over the forces of evil. Don't be deceived with evil communication because it corrupts good manners. So many of us were raised in good Christian homes, but the company we keep/kept, the modern-day generation, with its satanic undertaking, is constantly changing us, our family, our friends, and our neighbors. If we are to fight this satanic move, we need to look in the mirror, check ourselves, and turn our tongues over to God. There is life and death in the power of the tongue, and the only way we can stop the evil things that come out of it is by turning it over to God.

Always remember, evil forces will always tell you what you can and cannot do. For example, you can't get that job, you can't save your marriage, you can't stop looking at porn, you can't get a pay increase, you can't get a promotion, you can't be healed, you

The Power of The Tongue

can't find a good husband or a good wife, you can't stop gossiping, you don't have friends, or you can't pay your bills. The evil forces will always have you think negatively to keep you defeated and going down the wide road of destruction. When you believe these things, you will have a very nasty attitude toward people who have things and are doing well with their lives. Brothers and sisters, please hear what I am saying because the battle is near, and if you choose to be inducted into the wrong army, your tongue will be on fire for eternity. However, evil forces do not stand a chance with the forces of good. The devil will make you think when you curse or say rude things to people, you are big and bad and in control. But all you are doing is selling out to the devil for the time you are here on earth. He knows if you sell your soul to him now just to be on top and in the limelight, abusing and misusing people just for self-gratification, he will collect later. That will be on Judgment Day, when your name is blotted out of the book of life.

You or a friend may be struggling with evil forces constantly. If so, you or your friend should go to a friend who has strong faith in the Lord. If you have strong faith in the Lord, and you know someone who is struggling, go to or call that person as often as you can. Lift him or her up in spirit. Pray with that person. Read Scriptures together. Let that person know God hears his or her prayers and that faith is the substance of things hoped for, the evidence of things not seen. This battle we are fighting is not with flesh and blood; it is spiritual, and it is being fought against the rulers of darkness, the evil spirits of this world, wickedness in high places. So remember, love those who curse you and speak badly to you and about you. Proverbs 15:1-2 says: "A soft answer turneth away wrath: but grievous words stir up anger. The tongue of the wise useth knowledge aright: but the mouth of fools poureth out foolishness." It is time we all give one another respect through God's love. "Let no corrupt communication proceed out of your mouth, but that which is good to the use of edifying, that it may minister grace unto the hearers" (Eph. 4:29).

For forty years, I let evil forces control my life, and the sad thing about that is I knew the things I was doing and saying were wrong. Through all those years, the most amazing thing I found out is that God did not give up on me. Through His grace and mercy, He placed people in my path who prayed with and talked to me. If He saved me from having a filthy mouth, being negative, and planting bad seeds, He can do the same for you. All you have to do is trust Him and do what His Word tells you to do. Stop looking at and saying negative things. All you are doing when you do that is planting a seed that will grow. The bad thing about that is it doesn't always grow right away, but believe me, it will grow and come to pass when you don't expect it. Remember, good always wins over evil, and always call those things that are not as though they are.

If the people you are hanging out with—friends or family members—are negative and have bad attitudes and filthy (backbiting, gossiping, lying, and so on) mouths, change your friends, and pray for the people you were hanging out with because that lifestyle is not good for your spiritual life. First Corinthians 15:33 tells us, "Be not deceived: evil communications corrupt good manners." And Proverbs 13:3 states, "Those who guard their lips preserve their lives, but those who speak rashly will come to ruin" (NIV).

There is life and death in the power of the tongue. Which will you choose?

CHAPTER 6

LIFE AND DEATH

Life and death. What are we talking about when we say these two words or when we hear someone speak of them? Let me start with the word "death." "Death" is simply defined as the termination of life. But the death I am speaking about in this book is a spiritual death, meaning a separation from God. We are separated from God through the sinful lives we live—which include lying, cheating, stealing, committing adultery, killing, and putting other things before God, such as cars, money, or people, including movie stars, pro athletes, rappers, and singers. These are just a few of the sinful things that separate us from God; there are so many. What makes it sad is the soul knows and is always conscious of the sin that is being, or will be, committed. This generation is the walking dead being led to a burning grave.

One unknown writer wrote, "The moral character of a man's actions is determined by the moral state of his heart. The disposition to sin, or the habit of the soul that leads to the sinful act is itself also sin." James 1:14-15 says, "But every man is tempted, when he is drawn away of his own LUST, and enticed. Then when LUST hath conceived, it bringeth forth sin: and sin, when it is finished, bringeth forth DEATH" (emphasis added). We really must examine what comes out of our mouths because in reality, it is coming out of our hearts. So the question is, what is in your heart?

Note: *The heart is the center of all the operations of human life. In Jeremiah 17:9, the Bible says, "The heart is deceitful above all things, and desperately wicked: who can know it?" Now catch this: It contaminates a person's life and character, which brings about spiritual death, separation from our Lord and Savior, Jesus Christ. The bad thing about physical death is one can't be resurrected back to spiritual life.*

When people choose life over death, they trust in the Father's Son and are led by the Holy Spirit. I believe there are three things that keep them alive spiritually. One is studying His Word, meditating on it day and night (Josh. 1:8). The second is faith. The Word tells you that you must have faith. Even though you don't see what you have faith in, you still have to confess it with your mouth and believe it in your heart. That is what His Word tells us. Then it will come to pass (Rom. 4:17-25). The third thing is prayer. We must always pray, day and night. Praying builds a close relationship with the Father. Faith and obedience are what you need in your prayer requests. This will build a relationship. Don't forget, the Father knows your heart. I know there are many more important things; I just think for me, these hit the top of the list.

Following are a few things the Father gives you when you are alive in Him spiritually. He gives you His undying love, peace, joy, happiness, strength, and the desires of your heart. He fights your battles, He directs your steps, He gives you the victory, He makes your enemies be at peace with you, and He gives you life. The list goes on and on. This does not mean you won't have trials and tribulations. What it should tell you is He's got your back, as long as you are speaking life, trusting and following His Word, praising and glorifying Him, and believing Him. When I tell you living for Him is beautiful, believe it.

For those of you who are spiritually dead and want to be resurrected to a spiritual life with Christ, please follow these steps. Read and meditate on the following Scriptures day and night. I am only going to give you a few because there are many, but I think these should top the list.

First, you must have the desire in your heart to seek God. Matthew 6:33 says, "But seek ye first the kingdom of God, and his righteousness; and all these things shall be added unto you." The things you are doing and saying He will take care of; just seek Him with a pure heart.

After you have found Him, you must do the following because it is a major part of the new life. First John 1:9 says, "If we confess our sins, he is faithful and just to forgive us our sins, and to cleanse us from all unrighteousness." We must be precise when we confess our sins because our God is a precise God. Confessing and asking for forgiveness are one of the keys to spiritual life.

Furthermore, on confessing, I want you to read Romans 10:9-10: "That if thou shalt confess with thy mouth the Lord Jesus, and shalt believe in thine heart that God hath raised him from the dead, thou shalt be saved [have new life]. For with the heart man believeth unto righteousness; and with the mouth confession is made unto salvation." In Psalm 51:10, the Bible says, after David committed his sins, he realized he sinned against God, and he repented, and one of the things he requested was, "Create in me a clean heart, O God; and renew a right spirit within me." Please do the same, and ask God for that new life. He is waiting on you to take that first step. The ball is in your court.

Second Corinthians 5:17 says, "Therefore if any man be in Christ, he is a new creature: old things are passed away; behold, all things are become new." Please hear this: You will have the same body you have now; the only thing that has changed and will change is the spirit that is within you. Remember, the only way you can change anything or anybody is by starting at the root cause of the problem. In your case, you need to establish a personal relationship with the Father. It all starts with the heart. We must create a new heart because the Word says the heart is evil, and the issues of life come out of the heart. When we have a new heart, a right spirit is also renewed within us. When this happens, you don't say the things you used to, you don't act the way you used to, you don't go to the places you used to visit. You have been changed from the inside. You must fill your heart with new things, things of God, and start doing what the Bible says in 2 Timothy 2:15 and Joshua 1:8. Also, know what John 3:16 is to you; always know God loves you.

Words Really Hurt
I don't think we really know how much negative words hurt. If you are on the receiving end of negative, hurtful words, you can relate to what I am saying. These words have affected not only you, but everyone around you in some way or another. Following are a few things that may have affected you.

1. You aren't well-educated (you are dumb; you are stupid).
2. You are lazy (you don't want to work, are living off others, are stealing).
3. You are trash (you have low self-esteem, are thinking and acting like you are trash).
4. You are a loser (you are feeling you can't do anything right, are hanging around others who act like losers).
5. You are nothing but a liar (now all you do is lie).
6. You are a cheat (now all you do is cheat).
7. You can never do anything right (you stop trying, have low self-esteem).

These are negative seeds that are planted in our soil, which is our memory, that get in our hearts and grow stronger day by day. Especially when we were young and as our children are young, hearing these words every day keeps our spirits defeated to the things God has for us. Remember, a seed is one of God's principles—what is planted is what it will produce. If these seeds have been planted in you, you can overcome them by plucking them by the roots, and know that you have the victory through our Lord and Savior, Jesus Christ. Romans 8:37 says, "Nay, in all these things we are more than conquerors through him that loved us."

If you are the one who is always saying negative things, it is time you stop because lives are being damaged because of your words. Remember, we are all teachers and learners; we repeat what we hear and act the way we see others act. This starts from a very young age. As we grew up, we were learning and teaching at the same time. This is the cycle of life. The most important thing is how you choose to live your life. Choosing to live the hurtful life of "I was hurt, so I am going to hurt someone else through my words and actions" is not the way to go. Remember, there is life and death in the power of the tongue. Negative, sinful words are death. As I stated in an earlier chapter, this is a spiritual death, one in which you are separated from God, living a worldly lifestyle, saying and doing anything to anyone who gets in your way, not caring who you hurt as long as you get what you want.

We, as believers in Jesus Christ, are *in* this world, but not *of* this world. We are led by the Spirit, and it says "LET NO CORRUPT COMMUNICATION PROCEED OUT OF YOUR MOUTH, BUT THAT WHICH IS GOOD TO THE USE OF EDIFYING,

THAT IT MAY MINISTER GRACE UNTO THE HEARERS" (Eph. 4:29, emphasis added).

I know some of you are saying, "But I get so angry sometimes." Yes, I know that, but you should really think before you speak. When you think for a moment or two before you respond to a bad situation, what you were going to say at first will change. When we respond too quickly to something negative, we always say something we should not have said. The Word of God tells us, "BE YE ANGRY, AND SIN NOT: LET NOT THE SUN GO DOWN UPON YOUR WRATH" (Eph. 4:26, emphasis added).

CHAPTER 7

A PERFECT CREATION

God created man perfect. "God created man in his own image; in the image of God created he him; male and female created he them" (Gen. 1:27). What happened? God placed them in the Garden of Eden. He put them there to take care of it, cultivate it. He gave them a command to eat of every tree *except* the tree of good and evil. Here we have two people who were made prefect, having everything they need to survive. Then comes temptation in the form of a serpent, which tells the woman that she could eat of the tree that God told her not to eat from, and she would be smart. After listening to the craftiness of the serpent, which persuaded her to eat of the tree, she gave it to the perfect man, and he also ate from the tree. This was the beginning of sin as we know it today, being disobedient to the commands of God. You can read the story in the book of Genesis, in the first and second chapters.

These sinful ways have been passed down through generation after generation. And we still are not understanding the effect of our words on our generation and how they are really tearing us apart in every way possible. At one time, the words had us (and in some locations, still have us) not being able to sit in the same areas, or not being able to go through the front door at certain restaurants; the words even affected us at churches, in politics, and at jobs. When I read John 3:16, it tells me that "God so loved the world, that he gave his only begotten Son, that whosoever believeth in him should not perish, but have everlasting life." That tells me His Son died for everyone and not a few. We are all brothers and sisters in Christ Jesus. There is no room to be a hater. He created man perfect, and through our disobedience, we took on the life of sin; that's just what He forgave us for. He was saddened by our action against Him and our fellow man. So He sent His only Son to see why it was so hard for us to live a sinless life, loving one another, as the second greatest commandment tells us, loving our neighbors as we love ourselves. We fail in doing that. He gave us a second chance when He sent His Son to redeem us from sin. Jesus took all our sins on the cross so we could have a new start, proving that we could live in this world and not yield to sin because He did it, and we were created in His image.

In Him the power of our tongue is controlled. We know the things we say will be spoken to edify the listener. The point I am trying to get across to you is the negative things we say and do to others put them down, making them feel less than desirable, less than human, degrading them. Any of the negative things you have said or have heard you don't have to say or listen to. You are a child of God. You have the victory in Him. Put your trust in Him, and lean not on your own understanding. Rather, acknowledge Him, and He will direct your path. There is so much negative speaking today that many people are confused as to how to live the life that our Lord and Savior Jesus left for us. We have a negative lifestyle so ingrained in our minds and hearts that it fuels our daily actions. We focus on the negative conversation; we focus on negative actions and negative speaking. If you don't believe it, just listen to the conversations around you. Better yet, listen to the things you say. Our Father did not create you to take on the life of being a negative person. His Word says to call those things that are not as though they are (which is being positive).

Remember, the tongue is a deadly poison if you use it the wrong way. To get an idea of this small thing that is a part of your body, continue reading: "So also the tongue is a small thing, but what enormous damage it can do. A great forest can be set on fire by one tiny spark" (James 3:5, TLB).

Nugget: *Think back on one little thing you said that caused a big problem or one lie that had to be covered up by another lie. Or think about something someone said to you yesterday or even years ago that still has a negative impact on the way you are living, or what you said to someone that damaged the person's life.*

James 3:6 tells us, "And the tongue is a flame of fire. It is full of wickedness, and poisons every part of the body. And the tongue is set on fire by hell itself and can turn our whole lives into a blazing flame of destruction and disaster" (TLB)

Nugget: *How can something created so perfect turn out so wrong? Well, I believe because of a lack of knowledge. That little thing in your mouth called the tongue has a twofold mission: one that will put your life in a flame of destruction, creating heartaches for family and friends; and one that is eternal life through the One who controls the tongue, creating a positive atmosphere for you and those around you. The choice is yours. The Word says there is life and death in the power of the tongue. Which will you choose?*

If you can't make up your mind, keep reading; there is more for you to meditate on:

"The tongue of the just is as choice silver: the heart of the wicked is LITTLE WORTH" (Prov. 10:20, emphasis added).

Note: *In the end, what you say has no value; it is just breath you use to repent.*

"The lips of the righteous feed many: but fools die for want of wisdom" (Prov. 10:21).

Note: *This is what will happen to people lacking the knowledge about the power of the tongue.*

True Story

Let me tell you two short stories of one young man. If you have to read this twice, please do.

There was a young man I came to know very well back in the '70s and '80s. He was a smooth operator, or at least he thought he was. He smoked marijuana every day. He said when he first started smoking it made him feel so good. He said the smoke was so good he would never stop smoking it. Now, this was at the age of fourteen, heavily influenced by the company he was keeping. This went on for many years, even after getting married and having children; he was still saying he liked this smoke and he was not going to stop.

One day he was preparing to go on a trip with his family, so he had to score a "nickel bag" before he hit the road. Well, he scored his nickel bag, and they hit the road. Later that night, they pulled into a rest stop for a few hours and then got back on the road. He had smoked a joint at the rest stop at about 3 A.M. After getting back on the road and driving for about an hour, he said his eyes started feeling a little tight. They started closing slowly. Everyone in the car was asleep. He would crack the window to get some fresh air to try and keep him awake.

But that did not help. He fell asleep and was drifting onto the shoulder of the road. He said his speed was about sixty-five miles per hour. Hitting a bump on the shoulder woke him up, and he panicked, hitting the gas instead of the brake. He hit a ditch, flipping the car over onto oncoming southbound traffic when he was going north. The car slid about fifty feet upside down, meeting an eighteen-wheeler head-on. He believes through the grace of God, the driver of the eighteen-wheeler saw him, began slowing down, and finally came to a stop after pulling off the side of the road.

He came up to the side of the car and asked if everyone was okay. He said he had his right hand holding his daughter, who was strapped in. His wife had a small cut on her left knee. His daughter did not have a mark on her; neither did he. The truck driver helped everyone out of the car, called for help, and stayed until help arrived. At the moment all this happened, he knew someone was watching over him and his family. He thanked God for saving his family and his life. Remember, he said he would never stop smoking marijuana because it made him feel so good. Well, it almost cost him and his family members their lives.

Note: *Remember what the Bible says in the book of James: The tongue is a blazing flame of destruction and disaster. As you continue to read this story, you will begin to put everything together.*

He thanked God for saving their lives, but soon forgot what had happened, what had caused the accident. A few months later, the young man received orders to go to Germany, where he met new friends. Most of them smoked pot and hashish, and this was right down his alley; they were people to whom he could relate. For six months, he was in Germany without his family, living on the edge every day, putting his future and family in jeopardy, knowing if he got caught with drugs, he would be kicked out of the military. But the words he said many years earlier about never stopping smoking marijuana had become a full-grown seed that he planted.

He would go to work high every day or get high at work with other soldiers; he worked on an isolated site about twenty-five miles from the main company. One day he had to go to the company to pick up supplies, and on his way, he smoked a joint. When he arrived at the company, no one was there. He met the lieutenant, and he asked where everyone was. She said they were all at the theater. He asked why they were there, and she said they were getting urinalyses and that he needed to get his. He said, "Yes, ma'am" and got in his car and headed back to his work site because if he had gotten a urinalysis, he would have been busted. He stayed away from the company for two weeks, not smoking anything, afraid he would have to be tested. He wanted to clean his system of the marijuana and hashish.

Note: *There is life and death in the power of the tongue. How are you using your tongue?*

The story continues . . . . The second encounter had come and gone without his getting caught. A few months had passed, and he finally got a place, and his family was on its way to Germany. He was so happy, he set up a welcome home party with some of his friends. The party started out great until he became drunk. Everyone was leaving and going down the street to the pub. He decided he wanted to go too, but he was drunk, and his wife asked him not to go to the pub because he was already drunk. However, he did not listen. On top of that, he got into his car and drove two blocks to the pub. He stayed in the pub, drinking, and later decided to take his friend home who was staying about five miles from him. Both of them were drunk, asking for something to happen. (I didn't know about Prov. 20:1). Some of the same people I was drinking and smoking with were in church Sundays and Wednesdays, and at Bible study. After arriving at his friend's apartment, they sat in the car and talked for a few minutes. On his way back home, he hit a bump in the road, and some of his tapes fell on the floor. He proceeded to pick them up while still driving. Remember, he was still drunk. He bent over to pick up the tapes, and his foot pressed on the gas pedal, speeding up the car. He looked up in the nick of time to avoid a tree by turning the wheels sharply to the left. It was about 4 A.M. and still dark. Turning the wheel too quickly, with his foot still on the gas, he drove off the road, about twelve feet down, and into a tree. The car was totaled, and he had a small burse on his shoulder. He said for a moment, he did not know where he was.

A passerby saw what happened, stopped, and helped him get back on the road. His car still down below, his memory was beginning to come back to him as to what had happened. The person took him to work to get a truck to pull his car out. Then he was thinking about what he was going to tell his wife, who had only been in Germany a week. When he got home, he did not go into the bedroom; he slept on the sofa. One of the hardest things he had to do was tell his wife he had totaled the car after she had told him not to leave the house because he was so drunk. He did not know about Romans 13:13. He was a regular in church, but having a desire to please the flesh, and destroying his life and family because he was acting out what he said many years earlier.

Note: *Words are so powerful. If we really knew their power, we would watch what we say!*

The story's ending: After his third strike, he began to think about the life he was living and what it was doing to his family. It was New Year's Eve, and he went to a house party with some friends. He told his friends he was going to get drunk for the last time and smoke his last cigarette. He said he poured half a glass of rum and a little coke for a chaser, as they call it. He said he asked God to give him the strength to stop smoking and drinking. He sat in the chair and did not move for hours. He was so drunk that one of his friends had to remove a burning cigarette from his hand.

His friend took him home that night, New Year's Eve in 1983, and the young man has not touched any alcohol or smoked anything since that time—all because of the grace of God. He asked for God's help to pull that seed up from the root, and along with the drinking and smoking, he also stopped cursing. All of that was the beginning of knowing where his help came from. It was not from man because if man had the power, he never would have let the young man get that far in life doing the things he did. God had a plan for that young man, and that plan is to give his testimony of what God can do if you are obedient to

His Word. That young man is the author of this book, telling people there is power in the words they speak, and we need to choose our words very carefully.

Note: *There is a principle that God has put in place and cannot and will not change. Genesis 8:22 states: "While the earth remaineth, SEEDTIME AND HARVEST, and cold and heat, and summer and winter, and day and night shall not cease" (emphasis added).*

What does that mean? I am glad you asked. As long as the earth exists, these principles need to be recognized and understood by man. The one I will elaborate on is seedtime and harvest. When a seed is planted, it will grow, no matter who planted it. What's important is cultivating what was planted by you or someone else. The company you keep and the environment you live in will dictate your outcome. In the young man's case, when he smoked his first joint (marijuana), the seed was planted. He began to water that seed by smoking more, and before he knew it, he was saying that stuff was good and he would never stop smoking it. By this time, the seed was full-grown, and it was a big part of his life and almost took his and his family members' lives, all because of what he spoke. It was not so much smoking marijuana; it was what he was saying that kept the seed growing. We really need to understand that the words we say are very powerful; the Word tells us there is life and death in the power of the tongue, and if you love it, you will eat the fruit of it (Prov. 18:21).

CHAPTER 8

WHY DID YOU SAY THAT?

When you ask that question, nine out of ten people can't give you the real answer to it. Our society has learned to be negative and vengeful toward one another. They feel saying something nice to someone makes you seem weak. I believe all this comes from not knowing what the Word of God says, but what the people you hang around with say, or I should say your environment. Ephesians 4:29 says: "Let no corrupt word proceed out of your mouth, but what is good for necessary edification" (NKJV).

Not knowing why you say things can get you in big trouble, especially if they are hurtful and disgraceful. I am witness that words can hurt people. Even as a Christian, I have said so many hurtful things to people. And no, Christians are not exempt; some of them are the worst when it comes to this because they are supposed to know better. These are what I call word Christians. What do I mean by this? They go to church every Sunday and sometimes on Wednesday nights, and the only time they pick up their Bible is when they are on their way to church. They talk a very good game about the Word only on what they have heard. I was once one of them, until I started really studying the Word of God (2 Tim. 2:15). I know there are good seeds to plant and being planted. If you are planting them, please continue to do so; this is pleasing to God. We are focusing on cleaning up the negative parts of our lives that are being cultivated daily and that bring spiritual death to the speaker and the hearer.

I always like to refer back to Hosea 4:6, which I think is the root of things being done or not being done. I really believe when we don't have the knowledge of things, our children are learning from us, just like we learned from our parents, family members, friends, and associates. We are compromising the Word of God for political gain, money, recognition, a bigger church—the bottom line, for worldly, material things. The Word of God should never be compromised for any reason, yet we do it and let others do it too. We need to hold people accountable for the things they say, if the words are not edifying for the kingdom of God. It is a faithful saying: "For if we be dead with him, we shall also live with him: If we suffer, we shall also reign with him: if we deny him, he also will deny us" (2 Tim. 2:11-13).

Note: *If you stay on your knees with God, you will be able to stand and not fear man, because through prayer you will have built a relationship with the Father, who will protect you at all costs.*

Why do you say the things you say? Think about it. Is losing your life over negative speech worth it? I am speaking of a spiritual death, being separated from God. Many of you are separated, but after reading this book, you will see the errors of your ways and ask for forgiveness because you know it is the right thing to do. Saying and doing hurtful things really does have a lasting effect.

Following is what Matthew 12:33-37 says.

Destiny of Words

"And I tell you this, you must give an account on judgment day for every idle word you speak. The words you say will either acquit you or condemn you" (Matt. 12:36-37, NLT). The importance of watching what we say can't be stressed enough. The deceitfulness is a road leading to destruction.

Remember the story of the young man speaking words of destruction in life about loving and not smoking marijuana. That seed (words) was planted and watered every time he talked about how good it was. His destiny was the destruction of his life and that of everyone who loved him. Now think about the things you say that are taking you down the road of destruction. When I talk about words of destruction, I am not only talking about things you say to someone else. I am also talking about things you say about yourself. Some examples are:

1. I can't pass that test.
2. I am not going to get that promotion.
3. They are not going to give me a raise.

4. I am not going to make the team.
5. I can't sing.
6. Learning to play music is too hard.
7. They don't like me.
8. I am going to be laid off.
9. I can't pray long.
10. I can't read the Bible; I get sleepy.
11. I can't understand the Bible.
12. I can't stop drinking.
13. I can't stop smoking.
14. I can't lose this weight.
15. I can't stop using profanity.

These are just a few things you say about yourself that give water to the possibility that what you are saying will come to pass if not corrected. The more you say these negative things, the more you will begin to believe them in your heart, and you will never come to your full potential. Here again, the lack of knowledge shows we are destroying ourselves by saying words that will destroy our present and future.

Note: *The Word of God tells us: "I can do all things through Christ who strengthens me" (Phil. 4:13, NKJV). When you believe this, your life will change. Also, we are to call those things that are not as thou they were (Rom. 4:17).*

In previous chapters, I spoke about seedtime and harvest. This is what I am talking about when you say these negative things—you plant the seed, and when you continue to repeat them, putting all your energy into what you are saying and doing, it may not be right away, but that seed will blossom, and you are going to get what you planted. The Word of God is true, and you must believe it in order to live spiritually. Remember, "death and life are in the power of the tongue, and those who love it will eat its fruit" (Prov. 18:21, NKJV). All this is saying if you are speaking life to yourself, you will begin to live that life of joy. But if you are speaking negative and sinful things to yourself, you will begin to see what you are saying come to reality.

Note: These things are coming from the heart; they are not coming off the top of your head. They are things that were planted in the heart.

For the Word of God says, "But those things which proceed out of the mouth come forth from the HEART; and they defile the man. For out of the heart proceed evil thoughts, murders, adulteries, fornications, thefts, false witness, blasphemies" (Matt. 15:18-19). Now you know where the things you say and do come from, which were planted along the way from birth till now. As my friend apostle Evans says, it is not your fault, but it is your time. Here is something else you must know to fully understand why you can't stop saying the evil things to and about others, and also about yourself, which is stopping you from your spiritual growth in Christ: "Even so the tongue is a little member, and boasteth great things. Behold, how great a matter a little fire kindleth! And the tongue is a fire, a world of iniquity: so is the tongue among our members, that it defileth the whole body, and setteth on fire the course of nature; and it is set on fire of hell" (James 3:5-6). Then, James 3:8 says, "But the tongue can no man tame; it is an unruly evil, full of deadly poison."

Before I close this chapter, I want to remind you of another responsibility we have as parents, adults, leaders, and teachers. This is about our children; we need to teach them the Word of God and lead by example because they are very impressionable. They act, talk, walk, and wear their clothes like us, and I don't think we are setting a good example. We are letting everyone else raise our children because we are not teaching them at home, as the Word instructs us to do. We have to take back control of our family, but before we can do that, we must get our lives together, and I am going to give you some directions to do this.

CHAPTER 9

UPGRADES FOR DOWNLOAD

In this chapter, I will give you a few of the many Scriptures the Bible has for you to meditate on. I want you to think of this like you do your computer; every so often, you get something that pops up on your screen that says upgrades are now available for download. Just don't do what some people do and hit the "later" button; it is time for an upgrade, and we all need one daily. These daily upgrades help us walk that straight and narrow path because we all have fallen short and said things we should not have said from time to time. This is why it is so important to receive these upgrades daily. For those of you who are beginners, these verses, through the grace of our Lord and Savior, Jesus Christ, will remove the negative fire that is on your tongue and remove the poison from it.

Before I go any further, I want you to pray the following prayer. Please pray with a sincere heart because if it is not sincere, it will manifest in your life.

Gracious and heavenly Father, I repent of my sins against You and anyone else I may have hurt. I thank You for the understanding of Your Word, and I am asking You to create in me a clean heart and renew a new spirit in me, that I may be the person You have chosen me to be. Father, I believe I received the answer to my prayers. In the name of Jesus I pray. Amen.

The key to spiritual success is building a strong foundation and relationship with Jesus Christ, the Son. As you read these verses, please keep these five words in the forefront of your mind: FAITH, ACTION, TRUST, BELIEF and OBEDIENCE.

Step 1

Romans 10:9-10 tells us: "That if you confess with your mouth the Lord Jesus and believe in your HEART that God has raised Him from the dead, you will be saved. For with the HEART one believes unto righteousness, and with the mouth confession is made unto salvation" (emphasis added, NKJV).

Step 2

First John 1:9 says, "If we confess our sins, He is faithful and just to forgive us our sins and to cleanse us from all unrighteousness" (NKJV).

Note: *I have only just begun, and you can see it will take work on your part to start building your foundation and relationship with our Lord and Savior, Jesus Christ. When your heart is empty, you can start planting new seeds that will harvest new life in you. This new life will draw others like you, with the same spirit of new life, to you. If God can change a man who treated his people so badly they were afraid to let people know they believed in Him, He can change you. But you must yield yourself to Him for Him to do anything in you. (You must be reprogrammed, or receive an upgrade).*

Step 3

John 3:36 states, "He who believes in the Son has everlasting life; and he who does not believe the Son shall not see life, but the wrath of God abides on him" (NKJV).

Note: *You must believe in the Father, the Son, and the Holy Spirit, that they do exist, and they have your best interest at heart and are just waiting to give you the desires of your heart when you delight yourself in Him. Read Psalm 37:4.*

Step 4

"Most assuredly, I say to you, he who hears My word and believes in Him who sent Me has everlasting life, and shall not come into judgment, but has passed from death into life" (John 5:24, NKJV).

Note: *You must believe in the Word of God and read His Word, so when you hear someone speak of God,* *you should be able to know if the person is telling the truth. Please read 2 Timothy 2:15 and Joshua 1:8, and do what these verses say to you. They will plant the seed of understanding that will produce wisdom.*

Step 5

"Repent therefore and be converted, that your sins may be blotted out, so that times of refreshing may come from the presence of the Lord" (Acts 3:19, NKJV).

Note: It is time for a refreshing of your speech, a time to let God change your tone of voice and for you to be free of the bondage you have been in for the past few years. Let Him take control. This must be done through the Spirit because the flesh will always fight against the Spirit. You must trust God to do what He said He would if you give your life to Him. Read Ephesians 6:12.

Step 6

I can't stress enough how important the Spirit is to the believer. John 6:63 says, "It is the Spirit who gives life; the flesh profits nothing. The words that I speak to you are spirit, and they are life" (NKJV).

Note: Remember, there is life and death in the power of the tongue. When you say negative things to others and to yourself, you are speaking death. The Word of God tells us love covers a multitude of sin, so show your love to others with a smile and a kind word.

Step 7

I want you to read the following passage more than once, and read it from your Bible. Ephesians 4:22-29 (NKJV) states:

> . . . that you put off, concerning your former conduct, the old man which grows corrupt according to the deceitful lusts, and be renewed in the spirit or your mind, and that you put on the new man which was created according to God, in true righteousness and holiness. Therefore, putting away lying, "Let each one of you speak truth with his neighbor," for we are members of one another. "Be angry, and do not sin": do not let the sun go down on your wrath, nor give place to the devil. Let him who stole steal no longer, but rather let him labor, working with his hands what is good, that he may have something to give him who has need. Let no corrupt word proceed out of your mouth, but what is good for necessary edification, that it may impart grace to the hearers.

Step 8

A few more Scriptures I want you to read that talk about building that solid foundation we need are:

- 1 Timothy 6:19
- 2 Timothy 6:19
- 1 Corinthians 3:10
- Luke 6:49

Don't forget, the things we say determine our destiny, and the people we hang around will influence what we say and do. If you say it, you will focus on what you say, and before you know it, you will be doing what you said, or what you said will be happening to you. Dr. Michael Mitchell of RMI would say, "What you admire you will desire, what you desire you will require, and what you require you will acquire," so you need to be careful about what you admire. The same goes for what you say because the power of the tongue has life and death in it, and so many of us are the walking dead because of what we say. As apostle John Evans says, "It is not your fault, but it is your time," and I say it is time to refresh with an upgrade/new program download that will give you the victory in what you do and say.

As 2 Corinthians 5:17 says, "Therefore, if anyone is in Christ, he is a new creation; old things have passed away; behold, all things have become new" (NKJV).

Scriptures to Remember

Luke 6:27-28: "But I say to you who hear: Love your enemies, do good to those who hate you, bless those who curse you, and pray for those who spitefully use you" (NKJV).

1 Peter 4:8: "And above all things have fervent love for one another, for 'love will cover a multitude of sins'" (NKJV).

Why?
Why are kids doing drugs?
Why are kids selling drugs?
Why are kids killing people?
Why are we agreeing to let men marry men, and women marry women?
Why are kids drinking and smoking?
Why are young girls getting pregnant?
Why are there no fathers in the house?
Why are we so vengeful?
Why are all these things happening to us today?
Why are we compromising the Word of God?

These things are happening to us because we lack the knowledge of God's Word, for the ones who know it and refuse to obey it are being disobedient to His Word (Hosea 4:6). We are not training our children, as it tells us in Deuteronomy 4:5-7. When we train up a child in the ways of the Lord, the child will not depart from what he or she was taught. We must stop compromising the Word of God for personal gain and satisfying others at the expense of our relationship with the Lord. There is more time spent watching TV and playing video games than reading and studying the Word of God. There is no spiritual foundation in the household today. We are giving up eternal life just for a few moments of entertainment, fame, and money.

We really need to wake up and take a good look at what is going on around us. We are seeing things with blinded eyes, which leads us not to act until something drastically happens. Now, we may ask how and why this happens. Well, let us start at home.

Are you teaching or did you teach your child when he or she was young? You ask, "What can I teach my child?" Teach him or her the Word of God, just like it says to do in the book of Deuteronomy chapter 4. We must stop compromising the Word no matter what the situation is because compromising the Word of God will lead to death. I know it seems no matter what we do or say, crime, violence, and destruction of our morals are overwhelming. Some of us, in desperation, are asking, "What more can we do to take back cities, states, and the country?" We have been praying, and while we were praying, our country morally is still going down the drain, I believe faster than before. I ask myself why. As I listen to pastors and teachers, and read books, I begin to connect the dots. One writer stated, "Its only when the people of our world accept Jesus Christ as their Lord and Savior and make Him the Lord of their lives that they will change." Look around you; no amount of materialism, education, social reform, counseling, seminars, or new laws have stopped the typhoon of evil behavior that is drowning us with its actions.

But when we become true Christians and not just church members, we are new creations in Christ. Then and only then will we have the desire and the ability to change and follow Christ, turning from that evil lifestyle, living pure, upright, and truthful lives.

Remember, God wants all men to be saved, but I don't think that will happen until we change our way of thinking and speaking. I believe we are letting the media raise our children because we are so easily influenced by evil conversation, people speaking hateful things to and about others. We are too busy working, too busy on the computer, too busy on the cell phone, and too busy watching TV or listening to talk radio. We are too busy slandering one another and our leaders, and we call ourselves Christians. And you wonder why these evil things happen.

They will continue to happen until you change your attitude and way of thinking. You must request of God, "Create in me a clean heart, O God; and renew a right spirit within me" (Ps. 51:10). When we ask these things, we must make it personal. God is a personal God. He will not force you to do anything you don't want to do. But it is still up to us to spread the gospel to all nations, baptizing them in the name of the Father, the Son, and the Holy Ghost. This is the great commission that was given to us by God (Matt. 28:18-20).

Five Things the Word Does

- The Word of God convicts you (Neh. 8:9).
- The Word of God corrects you (Ps. 17:4).
- The Word of God cleanses you (Ps. 119:9).
- The Word of God confirms (John 8:31).
- The Word of God equips (Prov. 22:21).

Please keep in mind, there is death and life in the power of our tongues. We must watch what we say to people and around people. God loves you and wants you abundantly blessed, and you can only receive that through faith, action, trust, belief, and obedience in doing His Word.

CHAPTER 10

PRAYING GOD'S WAY

This is what God's Word says for us to do:

1. "If my people, which are called by my name . . .
2. . . . shall humble themselves, and PRAY, . . .
3. . . . and seek my face, . . .
4. . . . and turn from their wicked ways . . ."
   (2 Chron. 7:14, emphasis added).

This is what will happen to you if you obey His Word:

". . . then will I hear from heaven, and will FORGIVE their sin, and will HEAL their LAND" (2 Chron. 7:14, emphasis added).

1. I believe we all are God's people because He created the heaven and earth and everything in it, even man. It's just that some have accepted Him, and some have not.

2. The ones who are called by his name are required to humble themselves and pray. If you have accepted Him, it is your duty to spread the gospel wherever you go, saying that He is alive. Plant the seed, and he will give the increase. We must pray always (Eph. 6:18), "pray without ceasing" (1 Thess. 5:17). This is the master key to getting things done. Let me remind you that your prayers must be with a pure heart, having faith and belief in what you pray, for it will come to pass.
3. We must seek His face. I believe through prayer and studying His Word, meditating on it day and night, He will begin to reveal Himself to us (Josh. 1:8). Also, studying His Word will teach us how to divide the Word of truth. In this chapter, I will talk about the importance of prayer and what God says we must do in order to be forgiven. I know when we do what He tells us, we will be healed of negative thinking and negative speaking. Then we can pray with a pure and righteous heart for others. Prayer is one of the main ingredients in communicating with God. Talking to your father builds a closer relationship with you. Studying the Word and learning to pray God's way will lead to a successful life. The disciple asked Jesus to teach them to pray (Luke 11:1). God has laid everything out for us in His Word; now all we need to do is follow His instructions. He will give you understanding of anything; all you have to do is ask. Then you will understand the meaning of what you say to others and the things that are said to you. You will know the Holy Spirit

is working in your life because He will convict you of things you say to others and yourself. The tongue is very powerful; therefore, we must ask the Holy Spirit to help us control what we say.
4. When we are praying to God, we must *not* be selfish, always asking for things for ourselves and not thinking of others. When we pray for others, others are praying for us, and God is blessing the prayers that are going forward. Job 42:1-17 tells the story of how God blessed Job after he prayed for his friends.

Personal Prayers You Can Use

1. I am ready to take my stand against the powers of darkness.
Please help me to stand against the spiritual wickedness in high places that wants to destroy me, my family, my friends, and the church.

2. I put the belt of truth around my waist.
Help me to be a person of truth and to be reliable. Please give me the words to say when people ask why I believe and follow Jesus. Help me to tell about Jesus' death and resurrection, and His promise of eternal life to those who believe in Him.

3. I receive the breastplate of righteousness.
Thank you for giving me God's righteousness because I am not perfect. God's grace protects me with His righteousness because I believe in Jesus Christ, who teaches me all things through His Word.

4. I stand firmly on my feet, prepared with the gospel of peace.
Help me to resist temptation and stay away from people, things, places, and situations that tempt me. Help me to live in peace with my family, friends, and other like-minded believers.

5. I hold up my shield of faith.
Help me to hold up the shield and stop the arrows of doubt, negative speaking, lustful eyes, despair, and hopelessness that the enemy shoots at me.

6. I put the helmet of salvation upon my head.
Help me to know that no matter how rough life is, Jesus has conquered sin, and I live with the assurance that I will one day be with the Father in heaven.

7. I use the sword of the Spirit, the Word of God.
Thank You for giving me Your Word, the Good News of Your Son, Jesus. Help me to tell others about Him.

I believe it is important to know what we are saying and how we are saying it. Remember, we live by words; our lives depend on what we hear and what we say. Asking the Holy Spirit to come into your life is a big step toward becoming a better person and understanding what you are saying to yourself and others. God wants you to live a loving and peaceful life, saying things that will edify others and lift them up. Always think positively and speak positively to yourself and others.

CLOSING THOUGHTS

We can change the world by what we say, so let us say the correct things, things that will encourage, edify, and motivate. Remember, out of the heart come the issues of life, meaning what you say comes from the heart.

Remember the three C's of life: choice, chance, and change. We all must follow these in all aspects of our lives. We must make the **choice** to take the **chance** to **CHANGE.**

My Closing Prayer for You

Our Father, who art in heaven, hallowed be Thy name. Father, I thank You for laying it on this person's heart to read this book. Now that the seed has been planted, I ask that You give the increase, that this person changes the way he or she speaks to people. Please create in this person a new heart and renew a right spirit within him or her. And I ask You to continue to bless this person and his or her family. Father, I pray this prayer in the name of Your Son, Jesus. I thank You for the manifestation of Your Word in this person's heart with an outward showing of love.

www.ingramcontent.com/pod-product-compliance
Lightning Source LLC
LaVergne TN
LVHW051956060526
838201LV00059B/3676